CONTINENTAL HARMONY

CONTINENTAL HARMONY

MICHAEL GIZZI

ROOF BOOKS · NEW YORK

Some of these poems have appeared in the following maga-
zines: *Action Poetique, Hoodoos, Mandorla, o.blek, Screens
and Tasted Parallels, Shiny, Sulfur, Talisman, Temblor, Tyuoni,
TXT*, and in the anthology: *Broadway 2*. "Extreme Elegy" and
"Second Extreme Elegy" appeared as broadsides from Mad
River Press.

ISBN: 0-937804-41-X
Library of Congress Catalog Card No.: 91-061801

Design by Susan Bee.
Cover photo by Bill Barrette.

This book was made possible, in part, by grants from the New
York State Council on the Arts, The National Endowment for
the Arts, and other generous donors.

ROOF BOOKS
are published by
The Segue Foundation
303 East 8th Street
New York, NY 10009

for Barbieo

Today was my place.
                    —Edmond Jabès

One year was like another. Eventually everything would happen.
                    —Paul Bowles

CONTENTS

AMERICANA SCRIPTOR

Couldn't find myself they said
'cause I wasn't looking where they thought I should

Because I hear pictures
twigs tough out a leaf
—See?

'Stick one over there ya yellow stiff'
That view goes on inside too

But I doan wanna be a twig that growls fer leaves
rolling their song anthem out of em
then sitting for a big brown stretch dormir

Which is why I think
'I just got run over by a mind'

What was it I was saying
to explain to the world
who lives in the same puddle over one—
Each vision a suspension because it spans?

Best author I ever knew
was an arm
Didn't point to any one thing
just delivered the picture
like a Satchel Paige kinescope by rote

Said in fact when the voices stopped
'It felt like I lost my arm'

Gently I'd love to occur at the river
But I just saw a word
which sounded like a lump
and these are the mottos I have to endure

Behold, planter   a simple earth

Atlantic heart with infinite pleasure

Trace benevolence to human grace

Light

the asylum of man admire

And what with a powerful way of expressing
Speech   the natural trance in a man

Abundance breathing air of place

Tree who hath studying stars been to Paris
over great seas pitcht upon thee correspondent

A woman
every syllable in sober earnest intention
seizes us all

& methinks embryos hold ruins of towers
lovetalk of our settlements
huge forests peaceful and benign

Spring forward anticipated fields
Opulent farmers singing and praying

Seagown orchard peaches and milk

and whether thou canst dish them up

TREESTAINS

Funny this but I knew weather
didn't care a durn frame
of mundane footage for me
tho I sure shucks loved
being out with that galoot
I feel the eyes on my body
grinning monkeys—silly goof!
One needs a certain detachment
Who'd I think I was
My catskin windcheater purfled
with lincoln—that's jerkin
George. That's me
in the curtain blurred
with the meadowlark. I seen it
so many times it happens more
Trees leaves ocean all
as they're supposed to be
But then big brother nature
I brung you indoors said
have a seat next to the cookies
and still no cataclysm
From that day on the outdoors
meant more. Sweet neck
little pics in haze could equal
candy. Warmth from insight
such as this like shoals
of shawls. The world was
a grapevine flooded with tapes
I knew I'd never grow up
and that when I had trouble
a run in my daylight it was this
I'd lost sight of. No reality
buff born with his boots on
but battles. This isn my story
it's not happening to me I
haven't come this far. No

mystic monk with vow of poverty
just poor. I'd as soon chin-up
treetops begging help pictures
or leaf a kid with a tongue
growing clear up from his stomach
My heart's in those vertical chops
as if all my growing barked up
there

EXTREME ELEGY

after Ives

The Last Rites, *man*
3 helpings! Extreme
Triadic Unction a -bury
a -port a -ton, troughwater
with shadowbarn
               like mausoleum
deathward we glide, our viscera
slung The pitch
of New England the mind of an ear
shockt into blooming a -shire
a -vale a -wick   oaken
lid going to sleep
near still-
ness of my life—America,
un
writable love
of foliage in voice
     beside an axe
         'til evening
Canvas in moonlight an oversight
comin' up backstream But only
     a rheumy cache
              of russet spittle
like oaken funk, New England, a tonic

     a ton

REVIVAL

This angel goes nova
on Shimmering Ave I've
a photographic memory
I caress I look at the sun
but can't remember where
it was I want to cheat the dream
and run. One of me

goes straight to the sandheap
One comes with us
to these berries. Halfway down
my arms are shining and the leaves
under the wrists I even
take a speaking part
hear the grass grow
at the wrong time

I want to know for the sound
anyone who prefers the wave
I'm coming home to drown
and the dead who know congratulate me
sobbing in the lurches
the human pro is forced to scour
Unthinkable I hunt for them

What is this singing on the mark?
The last I see of it
is what I hear
                        Who of you
among the jury locked the door?
Tender
is the missing word. I can
count in my head
Even dead my clothes are warm

OPOSSUM'S CREED

Each time I cut my head off
the spittin image of spite
my nose thumbs screw my eyes
and mom's tomato potlatch
wallop pack is circus size
I love it when she smiles
and stains my lie 'The real
McCoy'd lay off that punch'

But I'm a Jesuit duodenal
dustbin (my true vocation
a jiffy lube) Figured I'd
lower the fahrenheit
tampering with the earth's
pulley like a sissy would

Sign above the fetish read
'descend' or 'descant'
Forgive minus deep six
under plus cross
Skull one more—
the screamin meemie is me
Another poke and Mr
Pal-o'-mine pantomimes bent

My mind's as tight as
the hair on that dog
but I crave enlightenment
like it was watercress
I give a boscage?
                              You bet

SUNRISE AT MIDNIGHT

I hate to say it but the sun has gone from solid
to stripes, honey-yellow and the dead snow
that bleached the corn in a rainbow of ways
You'd think you were playing Candyland with
Martin Luther King, that the sun
could sear the ass off any white boy messing
with our invention.
                         Vogue with envy
is fashion. These antlers fit me to a tee
Up in a life of birdies feeding on blueness
The lank adrenalin of my uniform gulled
into a confession spree: Every cotton pickin'
cirrus bone one of us wants his face
on the polluter's coffee table

SOLD AMERICAN

The greatest key to courage is shame
                                                    —Kerouac

Most learn early on
they're not their brother Tom Paine's keeper
jungle stew that strangers are
                            But we
the Good Joe   of the many
                    the gloms the fandom the weepers
recognize also   affluence
                                And wretches
there but for the dead n' living jitters go I
        licking sherbet from quietude
            to phooey overmuch
                                    until We
the Hungry forage trifle nuts
and Pluck
        juxtapose starvelings scouting in
the Dutch dollar gutter for a kitchen porch

Not to be exalted on veal *medaillons* you can
    bamboozle anyone deals
    Nor poached war whupass
        stealing Mom's apple pie at fax speed
above the fracases grief and dolor
Hungering under bush-edge
        drinking themselves sick
who have no Dust Bowl Co-op to get to
        no lynx coat better life
            of a certain sum
        no cab to Glades for kamikazes

So   where've you been Abuse
                            Pouring the wine Dim
        too much cheap soup
        for a gaunt sinking
There everything here belongs to me
                            Rain-bones

17

    relieved of a sea change
As you gradually starve
           remember the best things
   subordinate burlap sleeping free
    wilder in the film noir rain
a certain soupçon Franklin Club no-cash-flow look
   what paves the heart pond
     the one the flies buzz
       and the kids titter
But ah never mind
  they've good enough advice
  as far as it goes they have
   on the B flat bighand
                Uriah Heep Time
What's the use of making
           3 sheets to the wind
  Sing a song exhibit sores
  Sing a song ex a White Man

MIDDLETOWN / PARADISE AVE.

Rife day tiny caw
day lifting nude yawl.
Bull leaves honor mill onion end
commodity leafing.
Shady beaten love at bay.
Saddle dune or pace off Lent in
Risque Yuma.
Flower'd lair spur'd nectar pulse
included then stun'd   silly, buzzy.
Fen muzzle on lay maiden drips trout
nude ink.
In blazes lichen tannin belly warren
by alder.
                    Alto eagles waver

A PENNY IN THE DUST

I can see the red back-up lights of age
The tail they'll pull off my rattled cage
My last hours being hummed by candy wrappers in Mexico fetishes

Lucky you who does intrepid time

I don't ever want to eat again
The Song of My Selfishness

Think I'll have that operation after all
The one where they remove the dirt

My book and heart must never part
My lumber bonnet's lush gable's off

Hard to believe
I think aloud

The words line up like young bucks of youth hostile
I sign a paper waving my lips
I am the only original they

My front teeth in my back pocket
If it gets aphasic the whole town could go
Perish the thought

Or God could come to a bad end

THE GETAWAY

I'm a chicklet, shit! I mean chicken
Don't no never go nowhere. No road
I know the deadend's complaint by heart
—fleas, me body their foreigner
they already more. I even got a yellow
Go Slow Deaf Child Dead End sign
in my close-up cloaca. I've never
been further than the German Measles
or the Asiatic Flu (Shanghai strain)
I'm *scared*. Don't want to get any
of the world on me, germ whores
trotting the globe-poles growing up
lice-life on the scene to make me
and my ball to get rolling. Got
the picture? Dimmest then darkside
Billet of lading gives me the trots
but molten-in-place. Low modal, no
motivation to move from Point of Fear
Cape of Agora. Angora, I'll do my
itch of wanderlusting here, thanks
Just poke, say, like a spayed dog
sidestreet elopement for a bone chip
Arriva dirty

NEAR SENEGAL

for Barbieo

thought she was clinging there
as if it were
soft warm dusk had her
and this above
warm the river sparkled
him she was African
envy the woman with desire because he was
naturally a breast was words
but the last
how do you get thee there he shook his head
here heading north

•

door he saw stars for them
through a woman
say that she was
a curse a little later said of course
that only think it
said it's what you do thoughtfully
and yet a word have you ever
outside with a woman before but had a shawl
understand he fell silent
of course the girl lied again
it had been beautiful don't you think
suppose he went on the door
or whether she had

•

said it doesn't matter nodded
yes she said her head
hesitantly yes
one I was forced to
him she said that
good do you remember
no not so far
anyhow he did alot or did he remember
it seems sure and I remember
dressed otherwise I can't
said the girl bent forward certainly she said
no I think it was for him she fell
would you for me

.

anyhow he had him
self how much do you
listen he said I think
but that other man
his voice had grown inaudible
in what way were we getting it
after all that evening what had she
something she just said
quick she was appealingly as if
swimming and she met him her as long as you
while looking at the man
yet not so far as that
we can locate him as dusk
fell over

.

floral but so the picture was
paper it was a man
his head as if himself
the man him obscuring his head
kind the picture was summer and more than that
hot on the grass say
and they could grace when he focused
silence a wasp could be
sure but even so imagine
and then you tipped
this way you'd never said and he sang
annoy me about
every time I remember him mermaid
he wondered
full as he also had dead calm
with foliage

AT FIRST GLANCE

At nine drank three. Bathed
the back of nothing
in the mirror. The eyes I had
sounded mean doing a quiet
seventy. It was easy
drunk in auto tippling my own
dim man. Arch-mendicant
in this breezy going world.
Fun ain't it a little free
to gloat savagely. Smiled
her shoulder at me. You
who get to liking pretty
wear knuckles out thinking
boudoir tabletray *ubi sunt*.
Her dear white scut. She
with a vague scent and a lot of
leg art lighting it for her.
Reed by faintest breath bent,
cool. Play it clean. That's
all—she threw the switch.
Another boy palmed
in the cooler time

DIPSOMANIA

What was left of the pint
at a point. The fightgame. Abused
to my knees. I love me, I love me
not. Gangs in music imagery. Sick
of sentimental machines that break
in the night. My heart for one.
Pigtails gone to town in a wagon.
Bit of midd dist wood most rigid.
What was left
of the pint at a point. The flight
into Egad. Come to take this strange
piss. Dabbling in strange turf. Hugging
that halo copped in a crowd. What
was left of the pint at a point.
Ammo in situ. Light-painted plumage.
Tree stem. 19th century in moonlight
when dogs could sing *do-dah,*
do-dah. The more bedroom her eyes are.
Granted, every mug or mulberry isn't
contentious, it's a cinch. Bury this hatchet
in the monkey on my back. Habits
are qualities. A regular Joe
out of habit. Wear my logo, rummy
my soul. You're my beauty, or you die
tonight. What was left of the pint.
Mind? On the contrary, ghostly particulars

SEEKONK

Now comes the eye landward to woods

The virtuous comforted by sympathy & attention

Under shady tree praising straightness

promiscuous breed, variegated   pleasing

As useless plants wanting vegetative showers
invisible navigable silken bands

Embrace the broad lap
Conceive in woods men like plants

Space will polish some into rejoicing
Climate become in time as language

A river over liquid

our summer fields our evening meadow

SECOND EXTREME ELEGY

The lutel foul hath hire wyl

anecdote of eagle
habituated, narrative eye
as I know men, here, habitations
of men
better one send felon
than citizen
        breathe!   plenitude
from whatever epitome from nothing
to start   into being
       rudiments accrue settle swamp into
pleasing
meadow rough ridge to rural
song oak-bottom'd & copper sheath'd moonlight trick
                                   ing fish to tree
lux
ury erecting
dome
      so once
         this woody nation
grown fierce on winds
that fan a terrible
hunger
into rails

TECHNIQUE

That ain't no way to talk
sighed the Indian Head. *Verboten* by my Pa.
My hair before I went adjoined
this lobby. Males in leisure-laughs
a great desire to sound grasps. Tough guy
with cigar-eyes at the cash bar. That
ain't no way to talk. Wait a sec. Sat a spell.
Broke out my pad and penned a few
ventriloquist dances fast and wild
as lightning in fascination. That knowledge
of the edge in tones as she goes.
Deep back hillbilly's ill-fitting shit-laugh
points summer, lovely, in full swing.
About time somebody did that. Discrete
night tapping sound drank a brandy to its
chest. Juke-roar goin' nowhere—come 'ear
pooch. Nope. That ain't no way to talk
but turkey. Time and color precision a
match an inhale of harmony. Technique
is sound on the spot talk

SONNET

for Rosmarie

Best is the hearing of it all at once
nutrition of the moment shelf
sudden impulse musician
to one side outside the seam (the notself)

After a couple of misses
something that had been a run
listening for little cliffs
then one by one full of 'em

night curved seasounds
white barricade nor light
I said under my breath

there was bushes
at the back of my head
afterwards I thought a sap

PERSONAL NARRATIVE

First came the flagellants
'I win by being gaunt'
Built a booth in a swamp

and the subwaking self
ploughed under.
Turn up the truth

At the heart of the world
is the reptile
a mineral bird. My wilderness beat

They said of the man
he died a boy.
Drowning shines an idol

queer cuss in a crystal tux
nest along the mists
(My little girl Grace)

Cuckoo in the wild who toots a fourth
a deck of attention in the quoted
sound. Arc as a length of a clef

From the midnerve copse
A narrative
the object of my Captivity

OPERA MOP

for Steve Grob

What a bold rash coined a small spot after all. Nordic
Caprice. Periodical wind marking cotyledon monocular.
Ye grubber that casts up mold. Thought sulphuret of
stonecrop or livelong. Planetary expense, rainbow and
aureole. Nile-eating aria. Heard muslin whence it first
came and doublet music reduplicated rustling forms.
Seen from a counter the stem of a courtesan plunge.
Sang standard French bull 'Me do serenade my way' fighting
repertoire. Toughest order ever toned round I got away with,
Eh Toro?! F above staff, *gee* what a sow. Imagine
the life of a torso without a prayer. Losers
neath shiverin for. Never mind
how things were tied with rain, any tone you could eat
with a spoon but didn't. Talk about your moonlight
in it. Tune started key singing verses *but to her*. Mannish
boy. Spruce pearl nickel, lizard
in Mayan mindset. Say, I ain't fainthearted.
And yipped stuff the peer of the rest of it

OMNIBUS VERSES

for Craig Watson

I don't see any method
Say it again it keeps me awake
Wish I had words
That's my headache.
Little nipper at the padlock
Nooned and lonered.
I wonder what's a misleading word
Is it?
Some of the rumors were fanned on purpose.
That should put a spanner in it

Seen a furlong parboiled
Of parquet. Sudden parvenu
And the inner ear begun to
Flag. Further shewn by the use short-a-fry
Code name: Punitive. Goon brooch
And a pint of branches
Supt on a wood verb fowl, for the most part
Palaver, carryin a stick however small
Of myrtle against weariness. November
Loaded with sculpture
Without a word

Try not to react with glee. Your
Shaving brush of witchery.
They brute the town frequently
Finish your spinach, then
You can plate some bullets
Strop the nitrates with comely strip
Man has London on beef, centerpiece
Of Europa gallant. Juicy hit in
Dryform gummer

Mind one western mow,   Eyemark which
I've sent you talons I've had
The heads affixed.
I wonder luster or a wish
A higher finish relish? Memory pickles best
Robbie who wolfed and got dangerous
Chamber retort quartet.
Music ghetto for wind

I wonder what's a miss
Porno-wise? 70 quid and a butt of sack
Vernacular snatches I skim
With my doldrum
Hope for the image
I can masturbate
To, indefatigable doozy

GENTLEMEN OF THE JUNGLE

Is it true you cooked the book
of faux, how to eat your best friend
You son of a gun. Bang. Woof
Rollover. Play dead. These words
are coming through my window
on the sun. Every patriotic bone
one of them. How deep is the ocean
Give the man a stone. In the bloom
of his decrepitude, the husky
Eskimo amok behind his dog
knows how to eat his best
friend. Say it ain't so, Joe
I think that I shall never see
thinking *wild strawberries*
eating Jim Beam on the run
A cat or a comma
Pause or a coma. Say, Fido
can you Spot Old Yeller yet
Then roll up the carpet and bite the dust
Just a Coney Island parlor trick to us

Aboard my fingers to the fingerbones
This ole dog went strolling home

4TH ECLOGUE: TRANSMISSION

for Bud, whoever he is

I'm a loud, vulgar man. Am I right
in thinking? I've been feeling lately
suicidal, which is homicidal. So
watch out. My parts
of a flayed saint. Martyr
maybe. Deliriously lovely. You could
buy my heart at K-mart, maybe.
Don't count on my being there.
If we die tonight
it'll die with me.
                Virgil's real name
was Virgilio. Principio nut. Construction
bro. Had a wand the size
of a whipshop. My guts are
coming out and you want *me*.
All the engineers are bald.
Life ain't perverse. Life is. Ain't
perverse. Less Virgil's holiday log.
Foresaw Joseph Mary and little
Gigi with his little peepee
when the world was kneesocks
'hind hollyhock back. Life is weird,
wake up to it. What right
have I to leak the truth?

SOME SOUTHPAW PITCHING

for Bob Jacob, benefactor

1.

Damn it foxglove I heard a lisp

miles in the unmodified plural stream though in some cases the distances are hybrid, coined by German settlers. Right for the distance on this trail because it had a mill color of the water, sand rascals from an incident— Hardwood Place.

Note the confusion of carrying glacial silt. That's what I'm gonna call my land Milksickness 'cause it cries so to speak in the middle where duckhawks abound.

Community had a notable bridge and it looked like a good place for midnight. Gland gave rise to feminine as a woman late where the linden is not native.

President of a walking club three men called Joe. By jingo of batter toasted on a board haunted by crows. Where the echo is notable or observed in the water for having an easterly location. Mascot near this spot you could see was earth, pronounced wicks, the common word for beautiful in Fake Creek for the stream itself was honest.

Stretched some skins on trees confused with the more important cape whom the lake seen from a height was. Growth and a cool place and occurs in field alone and as a first element it is spelled felicity, grown here as a crop as a fiddle as being long and trim like a finger.

Water-sitting because the river swings probably mountain at, meaning lover of learning, ghost town there one evening rose from its ashes sounding words and those suggesting.

2.

Dinner halt on an early trail. Windy day resembling epaulets. Lone his last name spelled backwards. 3 tall pines shade the post office. An incident involving the game sprang the present town.

I excel in O! then vice versa endless by hyperbole. Works one of which was circular. CLARION the county and town vogue to that spelling. Jennie daughter of two railroad men. Clover reach to a straight stretch of the ancient water clock.

Brush anglicized as cripple a crutch and the letter O plied to a belt of wooded land running. Habitation with suggestion of being because in self-esteem a health resort. Whitehead in the memory of birds which has shifted current.

The gap in O.K. was the scene of a savage young swan. In basswood country an exotic name was used as a footbridge. A tree that is really a juniper of myself and other hunters in buffalo days.

A man buried here thus passing who was going in that direction.

3.

Then certain rascals went afoot cut across the neck to escape the odium of having their own. Bend in a river now no longer existing. Pep from the breakfast food cow outfit spilled much vexed the wash.

'a' ending since that is thought more. Grappling for sunken logs, huckleberry. Molasses to mean deep pond. Kilts for Jesse Kilts liked Chinese cook on private railroad. Motive in some instances of the numerous oaks.

A device for cracking nuts, miners named King and Lear. Most people was changed by folks. At the height of his literary brown hills.

Killpecker an adverse effect upon virility shone devil because of hot springs. Boy's saying going to Jerusalem hawked and killed for his furious driving.

Green with the suggestion of come paint stream to indicate color but later usage for a series in cinnabar. Dress to the inhabitants of Vermont for euphony or factory of enthusiasm believed to have been verdure a green spot surrounding sparrows to the namer. Operas which suggest a copper article prefixed for color.

Aid in the Revolution, half-brother of George commendatory ie very. Sighting of a hawk curing as a saint's name. Of s in the plural, twins in California that are not strictly speaking geysers. Tracks of giants being haunted by the ghost of a man. Colonial times. Mantown echoed mania.

4.

Pruning's an ancient practice to protect the public from unscrupulous stubs of varying lengths and the invasion of wood. Better than words is always a chance involved with spurs thereabouts while the tree is whips. Doing what I thought I was doing in another tempo.

Century slang word 'sockrider' come in the sticks or mist would have been enough. Slakes to indicate snow depth. An attractive view from the sight. Weeping where water drips murmuring sea pose. Wiser of the Lewis and Clark.

Local lumberman shifted by carelessness spelled in the county records female chief. O.K. from a colloquial call list ending on at. See ya.

Children were lost in such a mysterious book for a railroad station. Tidal stream the rest uncertain. Tavern where was kept painted there wind with mythological suggestion.

5.

Then spook my health which in your fuss must aspirin a tree. Presence of the now nearly extinct con named by punning upon. Aware otter was seen here that he had met with in his reading.

Syllables taken from Wichita Railroad Sound to a hair comb. Bucked off a box of explosive frontiersmen in a pinch. A formation resembling a woman who laid the town out.

Bones of that animal were found there. Furlong for you you out of state. Want a lift?

CONTINENTAL DRIFT

That one may implore   Another
to sway. Trees
out of a corner

of one's self. Like a woman
wearing a piece
of the weather. The way

language uses us
In the air there are
rumors of amnesia   Trees

walking on forever
In a single man so many
living hands

Like the kisses of
birds the rumor
passes

Unheard of
florescence
one cannot keep

as though it were a
drug for making melancolie
sweet

TRIPLE A

Everlasting stufft bird, lexicon of hints
at torso. Haunted bowsprit. Emblem of female
sex—whoa! nelly, just a Huron!
Get a Lariat on this tom foolery, bandsawing
the Bud! o let me put it this way AM/FM Galatea,
Colorado, you can hear my right arm up to here.
West Palm Beach poking at an off-center piece of
ice. Got a bedroom upstairs bigger'n my highschool.
Beam and whisper. This Mississippi River's
doggone deep and wi-wide. Baleful
exotic low bass booming over Gumboot Creek.
Chair window scenery. Seen brown gal Chattahoochee
Jubilee, jazz in ignition. Okay. But could ya
fetch me a duck from the kitchen Edgecomb? Echoic
isn't it? Memory of eminence over Jewtown. Scarcely.
Your Fanny's mine Laredo. Hefted. No more shining
big Leaf Mtns. Grog Run over Grief Hill.
Chinook mountain jargon. Lady halfwhite, a cuestick
lookin nervous, Miss Liberty, you gotta believe me
I didn't see nothing on Look Shack Hill. Sure,
blur the word, evenso, way to go D.C. comin through
the lie. And Gripe, Arizona lest I forget
Lackawanna, Moshassuck River, magic narrative gospel
from above. Onan origin of the feminine of hand
in the clear day roving. Bodega shot with feathers,
a kind of cognate in late corruption. Later bodice,
also a surname, highly specific: Clara Bird's
Nipple Tit Butte French 'breast' Mamelle *pardon*,
Missouri Fox. Let me put it this way. Transfer
the feeling, sphere of influence Thirsty Canyon
with head of woman and body to throb. What is
most lovely in railroad weeds (to pinnacle parts,
coin a phrase) eyes or navel? And it's wonderful
how unmonotonous they are and Dodge the saloon's
mimetic clams, an old cliche. Postcard from Prescott.
Curvaceous dots suggest eyes. The one you see

'bout a mile wide and an inch deep. Move the picture up
off the picture plane. Jokily help nudge attention
to layers of unassuming Flatbush. Measure
net gain after Slaughter in that Spirit.
Clouds and eggs went on as always about Flirtation Peak.
I never liked Soledad
reminds me how unalone I am. Harlem Watts Marin.
Get a yankee stem on the hymn. Hustle
ye sons of Harmony, Hominy, beardless boys—Asylum,
P.A. Once again retreat into the day.
From the tip of Potomac to the whites of Mount Vernon,
my men, not one unique. Not one alike.
Paid my dues. Reluctantly
gave up Widow's Peak, felt it
exactly in the button of my flank. Let me
put it this way, my town Stockbridge
screw the hydrangea. Obie ain't sheriff no more.
We drink to it. Me and him.
That's Union   *thataway*

STEM TIME

                    When the spark came
I was doing a gig
going to Rome like the song said, vision
intended my liberation
                        over the river
where sight swam
and as it were
                    amphibious, in the rose
in many of the coronary plants

                            Am I blue?
put your nose to the mirror
I was that close, bosoms
                        against
a panoramic hearing. Her ass
shall not inter me
                    I am old
So long
so Youth
            you are a state a remnant
of some wanna

Yeah
        and all that booty
must smother thee

SOCIAL SECURITY

Given nuance now give me deb
some iridescence
sing a short flutey lay
because she is not an eye
compare me to a day
proper sentences for each
and a starlight
like sops in dripping
solid facts, solid beef
dining substantially on thistle
crisp leaved young trees
an extreme soft between
dark stem close behind cottage
palpable tho faint
very high up elms fill
with light laid over
where shadows are to come
brilliant blue and lake
my disinherited errant hombre
section 8

THE KILLER INSIDE ME

I've got the butterflies on my white knuckles
like a Bird of Paradise from Hell
That's not with 2 wings but one X

Might I introduce his synthetic grief
at the invitation of the evening's goof
a shot of rawhide geezer back swill

upbeat dance tune about metamorphosis
Yeah, I refuse to integrate. I'm on a par
with the Express when the provinces tremble

I got bars as hard as a cranium's kraut
And that smile out there I wear
like a moat besides what is rightfully

mine when I give it to you. The winter
trees know my guilt but they're leaving
Aren't they. Feel the head flowing back

upon my tentpole. Habits like pretty prizes
Sexy touch of the many feminine things
My middle of the night stripe of manhood

What did you say to that poor sign
Who's shootin' who blanks, Honey
Take courage today attack is for rent

The point is not to return but get together
with Tex. Profession? Confidence
Your quotidian sport. Seance of ick the thought

a pittance. I'd like to die at the end
of your rope on 5 dollars a day
You don't know it, but you slay me

VESALIUS ASIDE

There's not much to a man
That ain't the fault of the melody
Something the river wanted to say
Strange, all I wanted was
The tip of her tongue
Derring-do does this to one?

Dear Ms Munez when I was
At the gym today I met
Anglo Saxon, the former 'great'
The angle is?
I'm leaving football. Also hunger
The deceased daughter of such Romantic endings

Of common sense popular as it's
Possible to be. Naturally
Things of another flowing
Company intuitively recognized
An era   the daughter of the voice
Barefoot, entering made a stream of

IN MY IVANHOE

Denial is a river in Egypt.
I was told to look back and not stare
Mummified in the classic.
We're all here 'cause we're not all there
Christ! wasn't a woman had him
Had a dueling scar, here
In my Ivanhoe.

Most of you were being born when I was
Icing this kiddo. Grim yore of grail-bait
Male medico squirt
Inner Templar Memling down his   shirt.
Soubriquet 'one-way Jack'
A pandy for the pansy says the leather of the pack
Did I say gramercy?

Continual chaps tilting out of kilter
Timber tremens. Flapjack in haystack
Sounds in the light of work
Curt *mit* laconic cream sung with migratory luster
In my panoply. Mowing an apish greengrass virelai
By my bauble! a moral
Sweet to me toenails
Waving pennon of a span scene.

Zoom cam to memory mote. Me and Pa
At the Twin Drive-In
Studs of the cinema steed
Parked car like palfrey, canted
Me more a Wamba than a Wilfred in my Dr D's
Brain-pan broken on Latin and gridiron.

Vassalage. Extensive wood in English song
Flipside spent hunting wolf in de Bois
To *Winterreise.* Grey-goose shaft of a gassy forester
This entity seems to dominate the picture
She thought he'd gone but he'd come. Summer

Being the chief romanceur couldn't
Keep his eyes off her. Bitchin' bodice. A real
Bim.

A cinch his off
Was on. A monk in his spare time
A mind's a wonderful thing to efface
It don't pay to skimp.
A look-see'll snuff stuff. Bip
That's it
No trace of M at the sideboy.
Nice of you to come clean, honey
Legend weaves her body yarn
In my Ivanhoe

THIRD EXTREME ELEGY

for Emmanuel Hocquard

A visiting professor of Anguish sore
    oarsman halfskullpain
        two L-shaped sections

the first the second hidden like the first
    one is fraught with mucilage of different voices
        drone of the hippodrome

too static stats
    repeats the six voices of the echo
        visible on the young singer's skirt

involved in the uptake of her peak bloom
    a run the bird sings in sunlight winglike
        because a waterfall falls

having had his camp here
    that eastern flow its buds
        and the elevation spell

a woman sundered that a girl
    experience a minute's intoxication
        near the middle of the cot

to the left of the future
    on the hour
        verse weather as main blooming bell

all told a teller
    a story as well
        after the last stroke of the brush

despite the absence of any lens
    that first pellet of noonday sun
        their fourth of Romance origin

as the last man set foot on the right
    his soul rose up to Paradise
        although no one else has

spotlight after iris
    this would not interfere with
        by antithesis already nicked by flames

BASEMENT & CO.

You're a guy things happen to
you were able to get in
her smile widened was almost
under his vest picked his buzz off
lit another woven rest
cooked up a yarn to protect her smile
being on slightly wrong

A guy in sleeve ends knee
deep in dead men the tunnel of roses
through his head thin and mean as spit
sneaking home coughs no money in the bank
and still has dew on him
mind if I look

Her lower lip between
her little white hand had fallen off
I tried again with a smoke ring
fished the glass case out nice
stretch of his hand on the nap of the rug
a padded rest and a tall misted glass
temple shadow the grass was missing
on the street he's walking
but his movements were pasty

Taking it easy I said
lying rubies she said owl my apartment
handle my key
I don't like it myself she said
he fell greensward
a human with a closed mind
lifting her eyes a nickel's worth

NOT ONE CENTIME

I failed as a Magic Christian being articulate
Sawed-off had to crawl back under my cork
Comb the microphone out of my hair
Weird as it got I wonder what I didn't do to get here
Did a road come with?

All my paints have 'reborn' on them
How not remarkable everything is
Now I'm back in line it feels good to be invisible?
I feint pretty well. I don't feel looks
All I can do is wait until I split?

There is no memory after they spook you
Of course, this makes the angels blind
How much out there is there peering through?
Amazing what the dead will tell you via stragglers
I read the other day someone turned the sun on in me

See, what? I look like I feel?
I've seen it said. If you see the wind
Call me. Could a rumor complete the equation
They'd love to come over and prove that they're folks
Autumn People who deal in novelty

You'll know them by their windows
Antiquated things they sun in their minds
Whadda you say that I should listen to without seeing?
I have a tongue, too, in my head makes speeches
A cleaner one. They never get said

See
There had to be a lesson in it somewhere

HYPER TABLEAU

Stood and deliver'd the daylight perks   Revved

actual scenery

Aced the tootables and a sheet of intender

Battered small whiff seeking grammar

lit a rag fer home. Natch
no cure for lads like you
Prayer and athletics? not enough.   Armor
ticking arson

Talk about your savage mind
Yeah, I'm the only one who hankers
The further I get from the scene of the crime
bleakness boxes leap to mind

I'd left a sign of Spring in journals
What botanists might call remorse
Slide of the scuttle shedding braces of
Summer

I never ceased whispering 'progressive sauce'
The fade of walks? depends

which way the wind grows

It occurred to me to grace their choir
nick scalp of angels then fuck-all

Throw the wolf at the door

I could see it for awhile
shelter bid with shiver pulse. A brawl

and a silvan stoop for brawn
An ointment to bite

With her own vim a welcome
home 'snack' as it were

Turban out of syrup jet
to recite my door

Snippets of flamboy breathe the word of gots
Noah in a prize ox. My ass!

even the lonely gets a voice
Thus spake Lucky the Pimp an Algebra

out of earshot
In league with owlers after vanishing

cream
Listen chief! disgracing is verse

B NOIR

The liquored up galoot got it in the labonza. I got it on the QT ahead of him. His bitch had a quim you'd dig glomming on to. I'm givin' it to ya straight. Anyway, dickhead bought the farm. He could jinx the luxo-meat off the hottest chicks. For openers who could help needling this knucklehead of his druthers. Shit. A load of wind happy as a clam futzing around when time shag-assed his trousers out of here.

Quite the quail she was, his squeeze. Who could figure it, figured it. I should know for cryin' out loud I bird-dogged the bim like she was my very own candy cane, and at dipshit's bidding. The skinny had him on everybody's dropdead list. Consistent.

She had a fudgy center for all her flightiness, plus stride and suspicious eyes to make ensemble work of her pony ass. Antenna of inside wit and know-how shampoo. I plunked down next to laissez-faire, I wasn't in the pillaging mood. A good thing. I was sucking at the nethermost tit where dead info washes up and thinks itself safe. I became the tinted one, passion gap, who drifts like a dingbat innocent.

Shit. Took me ten minutes to pack everything I had, including the expensive gadget.

SONNET: INDE

Everywhere the seam is showing
integer of tiger
every ivory it
and this in the Indian tongue is 'leaf'
all territory west of the river
become a thigh

Should the king slip through
wear the skeleton as ornament
of manhood about which
they sing at funerals
and fill the Plains with water
as it is called in the Indian tongue
the one you made me
the now languid wild one

THE RISINGDALE

A gardener's a bed book a pillow stalk
A dogwood text scratching
Taper on the pale rib petal. Vertical din
Helve dwelling on ahem
All sex aside then. Riverbanks
Tex, cubic leaves in oboe deep
St. John's emitic drink
Walt to the valves and partition. A hymn
In the horns to boot

First round draft chick. Sunnyside
Uppers. Mine of Miss O
Goggles that darting redound
To the dish, Alp me to a scribble
As I had hoped the face
On her hip but the fish got bigger
Beak conniving under balm
Southpaw at his sinuses, Woody
The shower drip geezer

Ring mob for a tripe rest
Study group of leaves more dignified than
Gout. Would I had ducks to stuff
Compounded foot of some fancied bugle
Cordaged in thicket in cabinet tan
Men in the minds of their women
Slickrock in a slot canyon
Even a morgue's got rules. Cremated
Fore we sold 'em on the sound

Musician diaphanous

ELKED BACK

After a benign grace
note the voice died
unfortified. I don't so much object
to its absence. Didn't like it much
by the way, the friendly
tone. The surgeon shares
to a certain extent
my temperament. Something so big
brought in a book of uranium
Sometimes little shafts
of wistfulness. Just yesterday
I went into the country, drank
that great portion. Nothing
happened. I understand this
note the blur. It's the promise I like
like oncoming traffic. Otherwise
I'd not've noticed

AN EJACULATION OF PHILO FUGING

Gee I wanna suffer Gus

show us those symphonic knees

interior definition of the spring tree—little fella
down a well

clutching a bar of acme—shoot! it were the surface
I'd a hit it by now

(a fuck-you-too in the text)

Momentum of maps after scapes

everything aside but national 'n pastime

Sam wags a greening plank weather thumpway

doubts then a dose then more sunt lacrima of molasses
or is it less but paler plumage

bonefish lies on the lap board

Geyserville to Goon Dip basked as a hybrid reading
'streamside wit'

I got the octaves to walk on

to stretch

THE HYPOS

A sunny day. My pants
up to the sky. Yikes
Maybe my heart'll break
this time. It'd serve it
right—trying to scare me
that way. Says 'hang on
grabass, to a tent flap'
and I think: I'm never
camping here again.
                    The only
thing to fear is paranoia
as if that weren't enough
also, eczema from stress
And everything subject to
fits of redress. Besides
the voice when it arrives
(a damsel in the A.M., tongue
in one ear, out the other)
is absolutely meaningless
Feels alone. Says 'Who
cut your throat and left you
boss?'

ABSORBENE JR.

Momma says I born you *the rabble*
My People
and the cleft chin on the pair of them
Never mind perspective
never let them see you dead
If you can't join'em
beat'em. Bad
Memos of the masklike
the netherhalf.

Who said the lyric's dead
that's me you're zinging!
I'll fill your mettle
full o' lead. Man
I'm a retread, don't want
one of anything. My god
had too much sterno
blurred when he should've blissed
Me, I want a new
tattoo. Acoustic spurs. Grifter's
verse. Time to fur the wind
Let's make a deal
I keep it all. A glimpse
and the mouths was something!

I'm not ashamed to
tell my name. I reckon
what they call the I, head on
with hood of worship
Behold the floor its tone
of injured wood, but there you were
Comfort, lip lob on the bias
Say! that's me you're zinging
See these eyes? they can
spot a priest at 5 o'clock high

Tomorrow we mounteth a paradise
pack your sighs

She'll wetter your wickets
ye lyric killers!

ILLUSTRATIVE

I'm becoming into being like awake camera
on rising street level under branch looking
past tissue to tree to campanile toward town
main street's end of. Alot like paint
can be a memory painted a picture
or field trip say 4th grade American Civilization
trip autumn bright but flat like paint can be
if too much oxygen is in the blue. Wait!
it's not October It's Spring
and the street is blue upsidedown
learned heroic histrionic history book light blue
that always reminds me of Washington, George eyes or
Washington, D.C. responsible for that safety in light feeling
American. Some single beaten brown last year's leaves
flipflop Disneylike down Main Street, common
the occasional limousine or UPS truck racing 'em on their way
to the now howitzer green of Spring
Red brick ain't really red red
except against a blue hickory book blue sky, a color
certain snobs like to think is theirs—Who's
naughtier than thou?—as if
the sky in a history book were a race of untouchables

ODE OF IT ALL

Like the kid who 'steals shit'
'cause he isn't worth the shit he'd take
I can't remember when I wasn't ashamed
as though chickenwire were a condition
I was bound to inhabit. Not even
espaliered apple of smalltown men's club
out back at midnight. The joke *is*
the chicken crossed the road
that I'm afraid to. The difference
is between the right word and what I think
it means to me. An oil
which is the function of my oleo memory

This head is no palace it's the Motel Abuse
It's guests are not welcome but disembodied
seep their message through the rocks
in my ear. The joke is they're dissatisfied
and refuse to pay for the room. How
can I evict them they don't know
their voices are the wards of my state
If when I sneeze I annoy them then
they're the only one I'm thinking of
They never heard but salty words
of a shoulder bird—their devil
was a crackpot

Gonna take a crackshot to stop this
bleeding. Moon like a cup—no, saucer
presses dawn. Up periscope: *shame*
a blowpatch on the plenum
I know by name

THE SHELL GAME

I'm mad as hell at your face in the sky
your imperial diligence, my carcass
in cahoots with your game of chance
I don't cotton to your fume of valence
nor insist you quit at sands of the parlor
Wipe another with nice
I'm Lassie-proof, Kimo Sabe. Miserable
child and all for a little equity
Probably an understudy was responsible
for my neglect. Say this
ain't comin through, Luminal Foil?
May nothing but volutes prime your pump

At a certain postern from the center I
appear in repeaters, seem to have
mastery and lie doggo. I'm
givin it to ya straight—this landscape
has lied before, wise and full of pranks
as safety in blue distance like
that thing there is no room for
My heart here but I'm still me
then south with the antiquities
your mind natters into

What you've given me the importance
of being angry is your wrath which
I telegraph back at you clearing my
throat tattoo on your phone's funny
bone now I'm in the know: a problem
with rhyme is reason. The goof of a man's
worth more than all his yes indeedy
One nut under three halves of what
you'll never know I feel trusting you

DREAM BOWL BOAT

Cockfight or coitus plumage balloons
midair scarlet hen when sable rooster
Espan american caliente extremes

In me too dream projector floatiness
but tough inside halting stuff
fishhooks in misty
'Can I get a witness' fraidy cat wayback impasse goop

Musn't forget Latino hothead message hook-up
muy bien of misfortune and the duende shot
accounts for initial mesh
of fuck and/or fight

But that red hen O
and Chicky she was a dish
the blood that sits in jars is not the blood in me red
That sudden ain't afraid of nothin red courage
is sex?

      In suspense
is animation in the mind timeless
the cardio-visual snapshot
'got it for all time' sense

Midair what had been atop bricko stuck wall
and would be   had to be   eventually
eyeshot alights

But not before passing front of fresco Rothko
like toreador door
or bull bumper of cartoon lore Funny
how it all comes
to gether like a wake

ROUGHNECK

Life-giving-water-damage on the brain
the friends I thought I'd have for Life
give my life for come again in guise
guileless of new friends guys on new
lawns and corners the same spare
rib Back, Simba gimmick chorus. So

Nothing changes. Not even me
So what's the diff? I should let go
in healing-waters that pray always
for me without me especially when
I think most *I'm lost* yet keep a-
going with wilderness shady eye of
doppelganger spooky creepies *sure*
'I'm fine, I'm fine'

Get back in line! your time ain't
come. But always comin' round just
the same at waterwindow bottom
of fortune-future eightball says
Ask Again. Say!

there goes Butch on porch, here
comes Clark on corner—smiles
like the Old Man did. So
the same feeling plays from eyes
slaps the back of new friend with
fervor of finding old friend like
'Friends for Life' Yo Steve!
Say Dave! Hey Whit! I'm standing
still. Still on moving floor of
Time so's not to miss you guys
Tender like a roughneck, long-
eyelashed, too, to catch every
tear I'd hope to cry to see you
still. And damn! I do

SONNET SUMMER OVERNIGHT

for Clark Coolidge

Elixir of logwood jitterbug of bling
'I have Indian blood' worn out with
Dodging that art in acquiring those
Berries of the citizen everyone wears
Deciduous droppings of a sentiment
Or seneschal whose aim is pellucid
As pone homey as the crosshatch of
Living lines where a body was or will
Be drawn in the mind. This here's
A study of portals the radio inside
My head peeking out from my heart
What was with what was
To be like older little boys
Dressed in a gimme no guffness

BAD BOY

for John Yau

I have a tree to turn over where being
thought of rivals *being* I'm bollixing
a stream of: The altered fish and
the renovated ape breathing sunbeams
Like a big guy in a little older boy
the eyes gradually migrate to the front
of the face, a bizarre disorder known
as neglect.

My cobbler suggested vocals. We've
become inseparable, one foot on a
blue shadow to breathe in some flesh
I'll be doing the voices, whistling
birdseed, the I-remember-marigold
in my six year old eye. A state
in which every cell's a citizen
Messages have to be seen to be heard
to say more what's happening while
cooing pictures. Geppetto's
prosthetic forehead punctuated by
bursts, invisible as the shock of
talk. So

the autumn afternoon roadside is
arranged, massaged by a wind of
fiction: all lies grown a *like*
I know it has legs, that now
I'm going to taste the music
A woman is saying 'torrid winds
tomorrow' yarning away. Weather
casting. Some little sun in her
hair and I'd have to water my neck
Now the overcast is taking over
I think I've earned this cage
in the world. A big truck made of
hard science moves the trees, the world

roars and the leaves point, handwriting
from a dreamtalk peels back dust. I
should take my sixteen hats off?
I'm the one who would never succumb
to salvation. No homespun haymaker
on the money likely to wing me, but
I didn't come here to get tough.
Besides the mind is bigger than
the brains I beat up. If you

find it in your heart, drop me
a fin. I can't make it on the one
wing, par for the course is paradise

Grant me the Grandview

THE RIPOFF

What she wants well who knows
but now she smiles *America* some
curvy silo preaching timber to the trees
that could as well sound streetwise
like no reason not to, right?
Any luck yet, Dollbody?

Look at your watch
when I'm speaking to your widow
my highschool nurse
of whom I was extremist fond
inoculating me with sunshine

And those horn thoughts sounded as sex
plumlike rounded shock effects proud
to be strange. Here
take this down: in the shape of a fish
her hair was

Suppose those spores lodged in the pores
suppose my eyes weren't running down my face
well, then I'm obliged and suffering
shining black light on my internal world
Look around. Wind says touch me and I bleed

Suppose I was untouched sorry flesh
some get along little recording angel
who crawled in out of the newsprint
to suss things out
less

LE CAHIER DU REFUGE

for Rosmarie & Keith

One a.m. or am I
Halfway through a shower
The demon tramp

Abandoned in favor of grinning
Coming home as a child
I was right at home

As if to say shall we
Amid so much mugging
Concoct a daydream world

And as a mime too
Shoulders arms forever
Talking dictionary howl

For our lives to be
Spared in the lipsmacking
Absence of the Net

That Rightness to be
Summer depicted the crowd
On my head whose

Dust in my mirror
As if we were one
Submerged in various cover

II.

Deep-rooted in short pants
at profound human risk
I settle for less the anxiety
I live with Leviathan
smiling on the inside wondering if
with joy I can ever get over take a breather

and wind a new life from this sliver (nothing
for a man of my caliber)

The mind blows taps my will
to be concealed unravels up a drip almost
as if I'd earned something 'My friend here's
gonna pay'
Take it inside, Rothschild
Beat it, Dust

I've got my own stopwatch heart-
patch of impending doom to swallow
Forget the dog, beware the owner
This boy just watches. I give up
a ghost
in the palm of my hand

III.

They think I'm something I think I'm
not, it's what I don't want so
I ask for it. This Sun
like a cosh comeuppance
for that moonlight

Now I've spillt the mind beans
can I be ornamental

Can one grow young in cruelty

Why don't the sick come apart

I wasn't too dumb to be like
Somebody Isn't night a hat

Go ahead, shoe! be important
But what's that under the talk you bring
Is some other coming wiser

Lighten up. I'm serious. Not for
nothing I was worried, I can't
sing 'sing' without the gas on

Who laid off some piece of my mind
your Rights of Man and
my human what is left

On the Trail of the Lonesome Pine

Couldn't we have another epidemic skies
Chubs of romantic gasland giving
pigeons off their chest

When are these insides out
No higher remarkable thing for this Kid
to confess

SONNET WILD TOWN

for Olivier Cadiot

What a view
Out of this world
I keep looking to see
If my zipper's up
My mind is blown
Like the Mafioso
Who sent his son
To Yale and he
Didn't learn a thing
Man, they got *some*
Eyes in this town
Good thing I brought
Mine, that Last
Supper's everywhere

CRANSTON, FRANCE

They bleed from the sleeve here, Ted
Just like Pawtucket
I don't embarrass easy
There's always something in the eye
Pour your mind at it and it opens
Right? Like a Fox Point (or Pawtucket)
An only -ville dreaming of shells
Under hog's magnet of men's sun
Or Manny Almeida's Ringside Bar
Sparring with the earth off Point St. Bridge
Pals whose knees commiserate
All I wanted was the water
With your hands attached
Monday morn scared as hell
And that's doin' well on a good day
South of Heaven in the deepest sense
I never looked at anything else

NOTHING BUT A MAN

I went to France with ants in my pants
That's right, fire ants! For it was written
He that conquers himself is greater than
He who conquers a city. I've got a conch shell
Here you might call a heart listening back
To that city there and those mates
Hell! why not mates, helpmates of my confidence
Given their confidence to me
I saw Emmett Kelly in the sky over Paris
In the dawn conquering himself
I wanted it all under my bigtop turntable mixing close
And heard trumpets because I know I did
And heard ants marching a ham sandwich I wouldn't eat
But watched eating their work up with my eyes
Saw the shiniest bare-assed homeless hobo
Squatting in a gutter bidet at Midi
On a tributary of the Blvd St Germaine
I was driving me nuts with 'Look! another one'
As though a hypnotist could ripen grapes
A brainchild stemming from a tree
What didn't I see
If I only had it whole I could conquer me

THE GRIFTERS

I so loved the world I shoveled off
this mortal mortuary soil a kiss
a final mint in with the infinite

Now nothing's convenient beyond
touching the earth for more
attention

Hell's raised ground level
for walking around

in. Like Death
I eat on the voyage

wine of addled Human Concord

Menace in the Royal Wood
My spade

in the long duration day
that knew how to dig a relative
or the kid in the heart
of a great criminal with gee

some glee. But I haven't got a prayer
except I'm standing in this box

blinder than rage with a bat
which is the national pastime of Love
And called on the carpet

I lie like a rug gene-mud misfit
clean out of towns. I didn't know
they came with keys, only libraries

of eyerollers. Their confab:
I fess-up in public to the lunacy
of my chagrin

Call me Ishkibibble

Maybe with a whalecloth hipcheck
in shark-infested suit I can
jumpstart some penance from

my individual doom institution

SAVAGE NIGHT

A contract killer contracts a series
of illnesses which spell out a message
Shame as a kind of elite
brought into the purview of a hound dog
Turkey talk, lipcravat of shoeshine boys
and the gas to keep going drifter
Pistol packer jacket pocket goes-off wraparound
some ransom money. Yeah
I'm the only one who loves you this month
In this corner, Baby Derring-do in diaper
bent so low his tattoos shudder on the uptake

Real Life is in the undertow. Sentences
stacked on top of that. Real life
taking all colors brown to the core
A rhythm set to the chomp of curs
The beauty of it (Love is
Strange) no matter how good she looks
apropos photography, it all
goes into razor blades Deep
in the Heart of Texas

TREEMAN'S LAMENT

Every guy up a tree has a secret
'No drunks or drifters need apply'
I got my part-time job
With the Distress Club, son, drool instructor
Save paupers from sparrows at the windows
That fear of having their hair seen
In pubic de poudre suit with a hit on their heads
And no window to throw it out of

Man, that libido bit's a death gig
Don't use just any words
Makes use of those meat nouns
Like coal shack night wind rapier trim
Words is like the trapeze rosin you'd wisht you
Rolled in when you see the ground rushing up

So they become the trapeze of the vision
Inhabits the space between your eye
And that console square acreage of your topgallant
Ticker waiting like a whistle for the wind
To blow through

And they fall on feeling, son, words
Swing there

THE FLAW IN THE SYSTEM

A profile's supposed to be a
skeleton key to a human being
Quiet birdmen near Terre Haute
their Chamber of Commerce sweethearts
Some come on soul trains
that been here before. Damned souls
of the air waves
              —Man,
   I couldn't sell wool to a diamond
—This hell is not a divine other
—I don't think therefore I am
Maybe you were somewhere
having beautiful thoughts
Time standing around
stupid letting sand
And that hiding place
in the phone rang

RECOIL

Feeling high off the medication feeling
that any odd action could be covered
by this exceptional excuse. Turning up
my nostrils at their edict
and the light switches of life proving to me
their shallow cover. Healing is such
an artificial remedy. A shingle breaks
and your mind goes with it. Downing dreams
like the red rose or lily hidden from society
Curling to be one green snake in the white wheat
Freezing, the deprived are one with all
never tasting the good life of no real value
Just sit and stare with no fatal blink
it makes you wonder where you really were

FOURTH EXTREME ELEGY

for Claude Royet-Journoud

Hoist sounds like grins bits
of ecstasy to get through Time
saddle the deadbeat's mirth
with deadly mayhem
smoke his eyepatch of color
compulsion his patron
a week away by penmanship
suicidal about Time
and God's light that bound his eye
to a tree shadow any
dream hand-hewn in a hurry

We have our own no two stakes
quite of white
where the paleface stray
makes homilies from on high
and flush with not mere slats but
dark playing The Continental Tease
brave tiptoe words across the bottom
thrusting through an ensign
a sidekick child swatting
with darkened spatula the morn

Doom is a slow dance
with will askew
in the nonverbal passing
of shivers these are not real
beam-ends but little ornamental
troubles achieving
a Fudd order of innocence
that mime the lost gizmo
into place and lantern
back behind that depth

Brilliant deed wants
to be American salt
the spaces off something
seen that barns you
toward reflection any town
midway through America
contains a Euclid
who spoke
and named the streets
remembered in France

FOREVER AFT

Up ahead everything comes to a turnstyle
A golden rod of never-ending wheat
It was my habit to take the wrong road
Jot my regards to the adroit gaucho
And Time being Time, disregard my arrival
You'll see in it the clack of an instant
I love the poor because in them I see myself
It's nice to be finished for a change
Didn't I say astonish me
Wait for an infant at the moment of birth
To persevere is a form of forsaking
I keep my senses trained on the shock
Absolve me from the greetings of the world

OTHER ROOF BOOKS

Andrews, Bruce. **Getting Ready To Have Been Frightened**. 116p. $7.50.

Andrews, Bruce. **R & B**. 32p. $2.50.

*Andrews, Bruce. **Wobbling**. 96p. $5.

Bee, Susan [Laufer]. **The Occurrence of Tune**, text by Charles Bernstein. 9 plates, 24p. $6.

Benson, Steve. **Blue Book**. Copub. with The Figures. 250p. $12.50

Bernstein, Charles. **Controlling Interests**. 88p. $6.

Bernstein, Charles (editor). **The Politics of Poetic Form**. 246p. $12.95.

Brossard, Nicole. **Picture Theory**. 188p. $11.95.

Child, Abigail. **From Solids**. 30p. $3.

Davies, Alan. **Active 24 Hours**. 100p. $5.

Davies, Alan. **Signage**. 184p. $11.

Day, Jean. **A Young Recruit**. 58p. $6.

Dickenson, George-Therese. **Transducing**. 175p. $7.50.

Di Palma, Ray. **Raik**. 100p. $9.95.

*Dreyer, Lynne. **The White Museum**. 80p. $6.

Eigner, Larry. **Areas Lights Heights**. 182p. $12, $22 (cloth).

Gizzi, Michael. **Continental Harmonies**. 92p. $8.95.

Gottlieb, Michael. **Ninety-Six Tears**. 88p. $5.

Grenier, Robert. **A Day at the Beach**. 80p. $6.

Hills, Henry. **Making Money**. 72p. $7.50. VHS videotape $24.95. Book & tape $29.95.

Inman, P. **Red Shift**. 64p. $6.

Legend. Collaboration by Andrews, Bernstein, DiPalma, McCaffery, and Silliman. Copub. with L=A=N=G=U=A=G=E. 250p. $12.

Mac Low, Jackson. **Representative Works: 1938-1985**. 360p. $12.95, $18.95 (cloth).

Mac Low, Jackson. **Twenties**. 112p. $8.95.

McCaffery, Steve. **North of Intention**. 240p. $12.95.

Moriarty, Laura. **Rondeaux**. 107p. $8.

Perelman, Bob. **Face Value**. 72p. $6.

*Robinson, Kit. **Ice Cubes**. 96p. $6.

Seaton, Peter. **The Son Master**. 64p. $4.

*Sherry, James. **Part Songs**. 28p. $10.

Sherry, James. **Popular Fiction**. 84p. $6.

Silliman, Ron. **The Age of Huts**. 150p. $10.

Silliman, Ron. **The New Sentence**. 200p. $10.

Templeton, Fiona. **YOU-The City**. 150p. $11.95.

Ward, Diane. Facsimile (Photocopy of **On Duke Ellington's Birthday, Trop-I- Dom, The Light American,** and **Theory of Emotion**). 50p. $5.

*Ward, Diane. **Never Without One**. 72pp. $5.

Ward, Diane. **Relation**. 64p. $7.50.

Watten, Barrett. **Progress**. 122p. $7.50.

Weiner, Hannah. **Little Books/Indians**. 92p. $4.

*Out of Print

For ordering or complete catalog write:
SEGUE DISTRIBUTING, 303 East 8th Street, New York, NY 10009